First published by Secret Quay Media Inc. 2015

Things That Happen By Chance
ISBN 978-0-9947957-0-0

Learn By Chance book series:
To order a copy of the book email _orders@learnbychancebooks.com_, or call 1-604-947-9283

Visit us online at www.learnbychancebooks.com

Creative Director:
Jason Bamford | Bamford Design | www.bamforddesign.com

Photographs by Gail Daldy

A special thank you to Mark Johnston for all his help.

Published By:
Secret Quay Media Inc.
Box 91194
West Vancouver, British Columbia, Canada
V7V 3N6

www.secretquaymedia.com

Printed in USA

What Happened
By Chance

While looking through some photographs of our son Chance growing up they instantly took me back in time to his early childhood. As my gift to him upon graduating high school I thought it would be fun to put together a collection of these chance snapshots into a little book.

The type face is actually created from some of his earliest hand writing in primary school. My hope was that he would be able to reflect back on his childhood and some of the special moments and share these everyday life lessons that he had learned as a child with his own children. It was these moments after all that made him into the person he has grown up to be.

Hopefully you can enjoy the book with your own little readers and with a smile talk about the simple things in life that teach them so much.

A Special Thanks - I'd like to thank my parents for making me aware of these little things in life.

www.learnbychancebooks.com

To Chance:

For affording me a mother's ultimate
pleasure of watching you become *you.*

Things That Happen By Chance

Sharing simple life lessons with children everywhere

Life is
always filled
with
little surprises

vaer sa snill   budakamnida   Kirpa Karke   varog   min fa lika

ripya   alstublieft   per favore   s'il vous plait   Kerem

please   parakalo

rolong   e'olu olu   fadlam   please

bud'laska   molim   snalla   asseblief

prosze   Kudasai   pozalujsta   bitte   ake

xin   le do thoil   lotfan   por favor

4   bevekshah   kor   doya kore   mghoi   os gwelwch yn dda

When you are asking
for something
always remember to say
please

When someone
helps you
always remember
to smile and say
thank you

dhonnobad mahalo moteshakkeram go raibh maith agat mghoi

kiitos dankie hvala lepo diolch arigatou multumesc

shukran xin cam on diakuju obrigato grazie tanvad

efharisto spasibo

xiexie

danku merci thank you terima kasih dziekuje

todah tesekkur danke

mersi ngiyabonga

tack gracias koszonom

mahadsanid takk kamsahamnida shukriya khawp khun

7

If you chew gum
remember 3 things
1. Keep it in your mouth
2. Don't swallow it
3. Never put it in your hair

when there is a job
to be done
it helps to plan your
attack

And stick to it

Until the very end

15

NO
I don't think
I ate
any cheesies

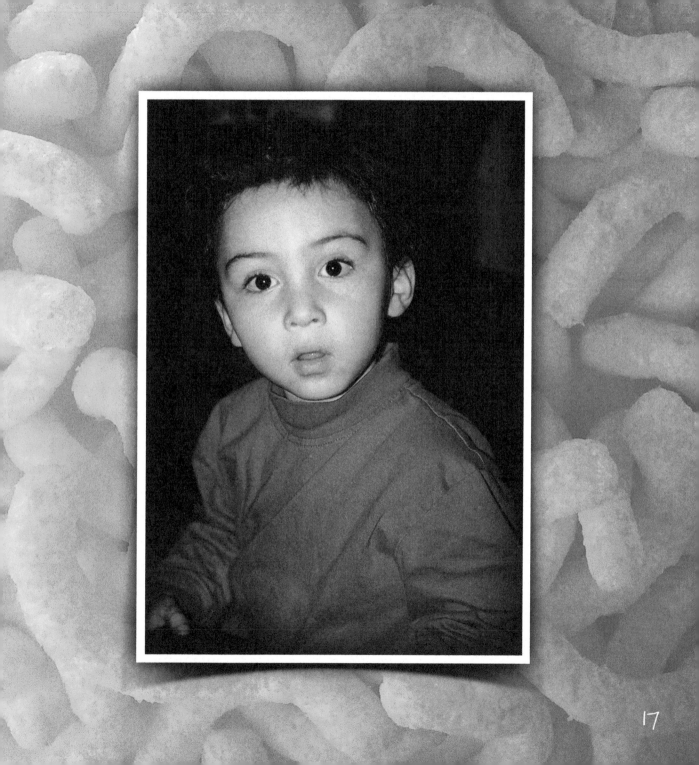

Feeding the
birds and ducks
is lots of fun

But don't forget
to close
the gate

you can eat
too much
chocolate cake

Be sure to
brush your teeth
every day
to keep them
clean and healthy

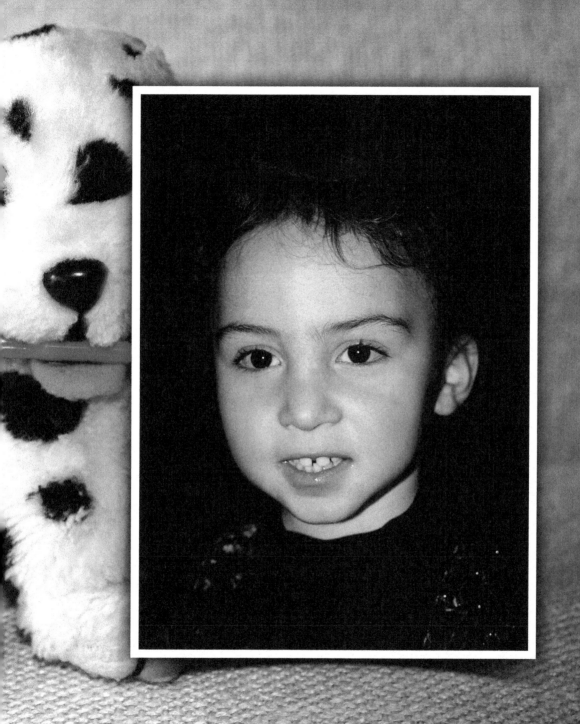

25

Always keep your
fingers
on the outside
of your nose

If there is
something you are
not sure about

And someone or something
makes you feel
not right inside
be sure to tell
a grown up right away

Wind and thunder
from down under
should be done
in private

I'm sorry
it was an
accident

34

It's fun learning
how to
bake cookies

Make sure
you mix all of the
ingredients together
really good

39

And always remember
to wash your hands
before
you start

When a friend
needs someone
to talk to

Always try
to be a
good listener

45

Never never
ever ever
eat
yellow snow

Sometimes
people tell stories
that are not true

49

Make sure you
tell stories
that are true

It's fun to
feel the wind
blow through
your hair

and the sand

wiggle

between your toes

Being nice
makes
all kinds of
friends

When you sing
sing
with all your
heart

Whenever you
get the
chance
just dance

Always
take the time
to stop
and
smell the flowers

Thank you for reading
my little book
and letting me share some
of my real
life lessons with you
by Chance

This is the first book of the Learn by Chance series.

www.learnbychancebooks.com

About the Author

Gail Daldy was born in Chilliwack, British Columbia on the west coast of Canada before settling on Bowen Island which is just off the Vancouver mainland. As a young woman she travelled extensively experiencing different cultures and everyday living in numerous countries.

From this she realized children are similar the world over and can learn from each other and the simple things that surround them. She believes this collection of chance photographs captures many of these everyday life lessons and illustrates them in an easy to understand way.

CPSIA information can be obtained
at www.ICGtesting.com
Printed in the USA
LVOW06s0017030217
523068LV00002B/2/P